NEVADA

ALASKA

CANADA

PACIFIC
OCEAN

UNITED
STATES

HAWAII

PUERTO
RICO

MEXICO

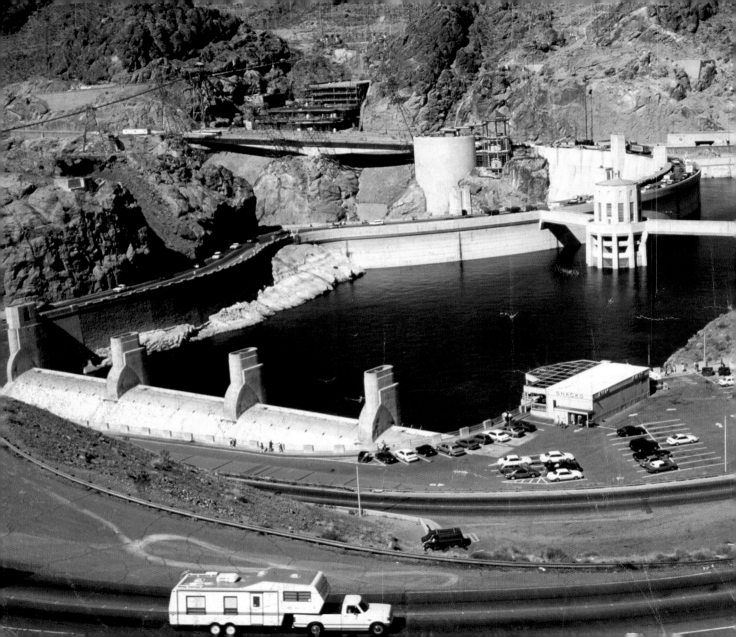

NEVADA

HELLO
U.S.A.

by Karen Sirvaitis

⌐ Lerner Publications Company

You'll find this picture of turquoise at the beginning of each chapter in this book. Nevada's state semi-precious gemstone, turquoise is a mineral common in dry regions of the world. Turquoise is soft and easy to polish, and it has been used to make jewelry for centuries.

Cover (left): Las Vegas Boulevard in Las Vegas. Cover (right): Rock formations in Cathedral Gorge State Park. Pages 2–3: Hoover Dam. Page 3: Beavertail cactus in bloom.

This book is available in two editions:
Library binding by Lerner Publications Company, a division of Lerner Publishing Group
Soft cover by First Avenue Editions, an imprint of Lerner Publishing Group
241 First Avenue North
Minneapolis, MN 55401 U.S.A.

Website address: www.lernerbooks.com

Library of Congress Cataloging-in-Publication Data

Sirvaitis, Karen, 1961–
    Nevada / by Karen Sirvaitis (Rev. and expanded 2nd ed.)
       p.   cm. — (Hello U.S.A.)
    Includes index.
    Summary: An introduction to the geography, history, economy, people,
      environmental issues, and interesting sites of Nevada.
    ISBN: 0–8225–4095–9 (lib. bdg. : alk paper)
    ISBN: 0–8225–0787–0 (pbk. : alk paper)
    1. Nevada—Juvenile literature. [1. Nevada.] I. Title. II. Series.
    F841.3.S57 2003
    979.3—dc21   2002001855

Manufactured in the United States of America
1 2 3 4 5 6 – JR – 08 07 06 05 04 03

CONTENTS

In Red Rock Canyon near Las Vegas, wild burros munch on desert grasses.

THE LAND

The Sagebrush State

Colorful rocks, darting lizards, and prickly cactuses are only a few of the many natural features of Nevada. Within its landscape and beyond, Nevada is full of surprises and wonders.

The seventh largest state in the country, Nevada is part of the Rocky Mountain region of the western United States. The state is bordered by Oregon, Idaho, Utah, Arizona, and California. Like its five neighbors, Nevada has deserts, mountains, pine forests, and lakes.

Nevada is divided into three land regions. The Great Basin covers most of the state. Nevada's other regions—the Columbia Plateau and the Sierra Nevada—are much smaller than the Great Basin but add striking features to the landscape.

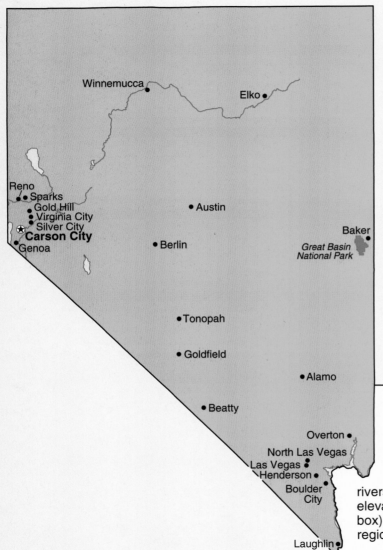

N
W   E
S

Winnemucca •

Elko •

• Austin

Reno
•• Sparks
• Gold Hill
• Virginia City
• Silver City
(★) **Carson City**
Genoa

• Berlin

Baker •
*Great Basin
National Park*

• Tonopah

• Goldfield

• Alamo

• Beatty

Overton •

North Las Vegas •
Las Vegas •
Henderson •

Boulder
City •

Laughlin •

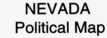

NEVADA
Political Map

(★)   State capital

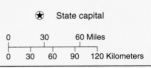

The drawing of Nevada on this page is
called a political map. It shows features
created by people, including cities and
parks. The map on the facing page is
called a physical map. It shows physical
features of Nevada, such as mountains,
rivers, and lakes. The colors represent a range of
elevations, or heights above sea level (see legend
box). This map also shows the geographical
regions of Nevada.

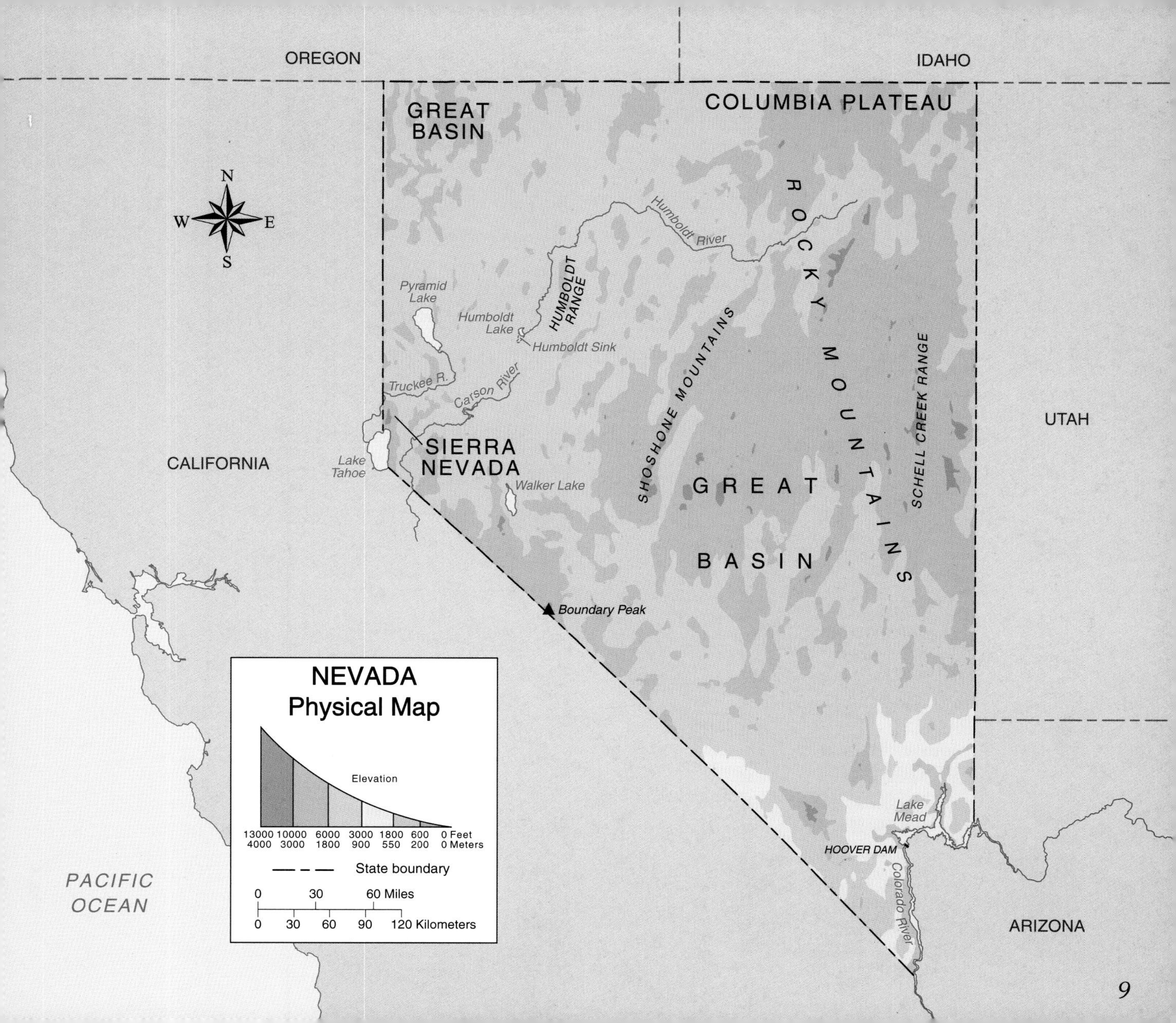

OREGON

IDAHO

GREAT
BASIN

COLUMBIA PLATEAU

Humboldt River

R
O
C
K
Y

M
O
U
N
T
A
I
N
S

*Pyramid
Lake*

HUMBOLDT
RANGE

*Humboldt
Lake*

Humboldt Sink

SHOSHONE MOUNTAINS

SCHELL CREEK RANGE

UTAH

Truckee R.

Carson River

SIERRA
NEVADA

CALIFORNIA

*Lake
Tahoe*

Walker Lake

G R E A T

B A S I N

▲ *Boundary Peak*

*Lake
Mead*

HOOVER DAM

PACIFIC
OCEAN

Colorado River

ARIZONA

NEVADA
Physical Map

Elevation

| 13000 | 10000 | 6000 | 3000 | 1800 | 600 | 0 Feet |
| 4000 | 3000 | 1800 | 900 | 550 | 200 | 0 Meters |

— — — State boundary

| 0 | | 30 | | 60 Miles |

| 0 | 30 | 60 | 90 | 120 Kilometers |

9

Much of the Great Basin is **desert,** or dry land, and mountain ranges. Nevada's Great Basin is part of a much larger region that spans several states. The basin is shaped somewhat like a large shallow bowl—that is, the region is higher around the edges and lower in the center. As a result, many of the Great Basin's rivers drain inward instead of up and out toward the sea.

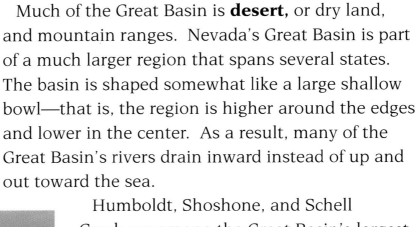

Desert shrubs and grasses grow throughout parts of the Great Basin.

Humboldt, Shoshone, and Schell Creek are among the Great Basin's largest mountain ranges. Pine trees blanket some of the slopes. **Mesas,** or flat-topped hills, and valleys separate the ranges.

The Columbia Plateau region of northeastern Nevada lies on top of hardened **lava.** Thousands of years ago, hot, liquid lava, or melted rock, seeped up from deep within the earth's crust and spread over the land. As it cooled, the lava turned into rock, creating a **plateau,** or flat highland. Over thousands of years, rivers cut deep gorges into the plateau, forming canyons.

Pine trees cover
many of Nevada's
mountain slopes.

A popular tourist attraction, Lake Tahoe is 22 miles long and 1,685 feet deep.

The Sierra Nevada is a mountain range extending 400 miles north to south along part of eastern California. A short stretch of the range crosses into western Nevada, forming the state's third region. A few lakes dot the state's Sierra Nevada region. Lake Tahoe, a popular vacation spot, straddles Nevada's border with California.

About one-tenth of Nevada was once buried under a gigantic lake known as Lahontan. Over thousands of years, Lahontan dried up almost completely, leaving only the much smaller Pyramid Lake and Walker Lake in western Nevada. Pyramid Lake is the only lake in the world to harbor the ancient cui-ui, a kind of fish that has managed to survive many changes in its environment.

Lake Mead is Nevada's largest **reservoir,** or artificial lake. At 247 square miles, Lake Mead is also one of the largest reservoirs in the world. The lake was created when workers built the Hoover Dam in 1936 to control the flow of the Colorado River in southeastern Nevada.

The Colorado River defines most of Nevada's border with Arizona. Some other major waterways in the state include the Truckee and Humboldt Rivers. The Truckee winds from Lake Tahoe down into Pyramid Lake. Farther north, the Humboldt River flows west into Humboldt Lake.

Hoover Dam, one of the world's tallest concrete dams, controls the flow of the Colorado River.

Seasons and temperatures vary in Nevada. Southern Nevada has long, hot summers and short, mild winters. Summer temperatures average 86° F, with daytime temperatures often above 100° F. Winter temperatures seldom drop below freezing (32° F). In the northern part of the state, summers are also hot, but winters bring temperatures averaging 24° F.

Most of the state gets very little snow, but each year the Sierra Nevada region receives up to 25 inches. In Spanish, the word *nevada* means "snow-clad." Nevada takes its name from these mountains.

Nevada is the driest of the 50 states. An average of only 9 inches of **precipitation** (rain, snow, sleet, and hail) falls in Nevada each year. Because the state can get so dry and

Nevada takes its name from the snow-covered Sierra Nevada.

hot, some bodies of water in Nevada—including Humboldt Lake and part of the Humboldt River— dry up during the summer.

When rain does appear, it is sometimes dramatic, causing a **flash flood**. This usually happens once or twice a year, when a brief thunderstorm pounds the desert. Rushing rainwater carries sand downhill, forming a channel. As the channel widens, more water travels faster and faster, washing away almost everything in its path.

The amount of rain that falls in the desert can support only the hardiest of plants. Sagebrush, which smells of sweet sage but tastes bitter, needs little water to survive. This bushy plant thrives in the state's deserts, earning Nevada one of its nicknames—the Sagebrush State. Desert conditions are also ideal for cactuses, which are able to store water in their stems.

Forests of aspen and pine cover Nevada's mountainsides. Willows and cottonwoods line riverbanks. Wildflowers such as violets and Indian paintbrushes bloom in the state's meadows during the spring.

A wild burro *(right)* roams through Rhyolite, one of Nevada's many ghost towns. Nevada's state bird is the mountain bluebird *(below)*.

Large animals found in Nevada include mule deer, pronghorn antelope, and bighorn sheep. The sure-footed bighorn lives high in the mountains, where its enemies find the steep slopes too dangerous to tread. Bands of wild horses and of burros run throughout the state, and badgers and porcupines scuttle about. Nevada's lakes and rivers carry an abundance of trout and bass.

THE HISTORY

Striking It Rich

eyond this place there be dragons." That's how mapmakers first described Nevada's Great Basin. Crossing the dry, sun-scorched desert meant certain death for anyone who dared try. These European explorers did not know how to find food and water in the desert. But they would learn from the Indians, as the Indians had learned from their ancestors.

The colorful Indian paintbrush is found in much of western North America, including Nevada. It gets its name from the legend of an Indian boy who painted a vivid sunset and left his paintbrushes behind on the ground. The next morning, the hillside was filled with beautiful flowers where his paintbrushes had lain.

The first peoples to enter Nevada's Great Basin probably arrived about 12,000 years ago. These Indians, or Native Americans, gathered seeds and roots for food. They moved around the region, hunting animals and gathering seasonal foods. By about A.D. 100, they had begun to grow some of their food near rivers, using tools to plant crops.

These people became known as the Basket Makers because they made baskets and other items from dried grasses. The Basket Makers wove their containers tight enough to hold water. By placing sun-baked rocks, seeds, and water into a basket, the Indians made a hot soup.

Around the year 750, the Basket Makers started channeling water from rivers and streams to their crops. This process, called **irrigation,** was important for people trying to survive in the dry Great Basin. With well-watered crops, the Basket Makers could grow more food.

Their harvests were plentiful, and the Basket Makers no longer needed to move around the region searching for food. Using clay, they built flat-roofed

Early Indian inhabitants learned to thrive in the harsh environment of Nevada's Great Basin. The first European explorers risked their lives to cross it.

houses called **pueblos.** The Basket Makers who lived in these homes eventually became known as the Pueblo Indians.

This artwork shows Pueblo Indians celebrating the harvest.

In what later became the southeastern corner of Nevada, the Pueblo Indians built a large city known as Pueblo Grande de Nevada. At one time, the community may have had as many as 20,000 residents. People farmed, hunted, mined, and traded with other Indian groups.

Pueblo Grande is also known as the Lost City, and it could be called Nevada's first **ghost town.** By the year 1150, the Pueblo Indians had abandoned the city and the rest of the Great Basin. No one knows for certain why.

This pueblo is part of the ancient Indian city of Pueblo Grande de Nevada.

At about the same time, other groups of Indians were moving into the Great Basin. The largest tribes were the Shoshone, the Paiute, and the Washo. Unlike the Pueblo Indians, the newcomers moved from place to place, hunting animals and gathering most of their foods from the wild.

The Paiute Indians roamed Nevada's Great Basin area in search of food. Their temporary villages were made of shelters that could be easily constructed.

Because they moved often, these Indians built temporary shelters. Each family took care of its own needs, making sure to have enough food and clothing for itself. Small villages existed, and each had a leader. The village leader sometimes organized rabbit and antelope hunts, or the yearly harvest of pine nuts. But the leader had little control over the daily lives of the people.

Indians living in the deserts of the Great Basin probably had little contact with explorers and fur trappers who began to arrive in the area from Britain and the United States in the early 1800s. At the time, the United States was a new nation whose borders were on the eastern coast of North America.

In 1826 Peter Skene Ogden of the Hudson's Bay Company entered what later became northeastern Nevada. The same year, Jedediah Strong Smith of the Rocky Mountain Fur Company followed the Colorado River into southern Nevada. Both men were looking for something worth a lot of money—beavers.

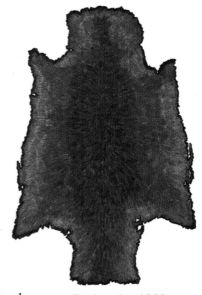

During the 1800s, beaver pelts like this one were made into fashionable hats or coats.

Fur trappers in North America often got rich selling pelts to customers in Europe and Asia, where beaver hats were popular. Searching for beavers, Ogden and Smith led their tired and hungry parties through mountain snowstorms and across blistering deserts in the Nevada area.

In the years to come, Smith and Ogden returned to the region. They brought other fur trappers and befriended the Indians, who helped the newcomers find food and water in the desert. Smith and Ogden did not find as many beavers as they had hoped to, and few people came to the Great Basin.

But something happened in 1848 that caused more than 300,000 people to brave Nevada's deserts and mountains—the California gold rush.

To reach the gold in California, miners crossed the Great Basin on trails that had been mapped out by Smith, Ogden, and other explorers. Many travelers followed the Humboldt River. Some of these people chose to stay in Nevada. Most of those who remained were Mormons, or members of the Church of Jesus Christ of Latter-day Saints.

Miners in the 1850s could buy and sell goods at the Mormon trading post in Genoa.

In 1851 the Mormons set up a trading post near the California-Nevada border and sold supplies to miners. These Mormons built homes and planted and irrigated crops. Non-Mormons also came to live near the trading post. It grew into Genoa, the first town settled by white people in Nevada.

The Mormons left Genoa in 1857. That year church leaders called all Mormons to Salt Lake City, Utah, to fight in the Mormon War. Few settlers remained in Nevada in 1859, when two miners discovered silver and gold in western Nevada.

Thousands of miners moved to western Nevada in the 1860s to mine the Comstock Lode *(right)*. They lived in tents or stone huts until several towns were built. The largest mining town was Virginia City *(opposite page)*.

The discovery, named the Comstock Lode, lured thousands of fortune seekers to the mines. The rich deposits of silver made some people millionaires. Others unknowingly sold their mining claims for much less than they were worth. Still others lost their fortunes in poker games or to thieves.

Wealthy miners built Silver City, Gold Hill, and Virginia City. With thousands of residents, Virginia City quickly became the largest and busiest town in Nevada. It boasted mansions, first-class hotels, and more than 100 saloons. It was also home to the *Territorial Enterprise*, the newspaper where writer Mark Twain began his career.

In 1861 the Northern and Southern states began fighting each other in the Civil War. That same year, the U.S. government created the Nevada Territory. Abraham Lincoln, the president of the United States, wanted Nevada to become a state. Most Nevadans supported Lincoln and the Northern states, also known as the Union.

By making Nevada a state, Lincoln could use its silver and gold to pay the Union's war costs. He could also keep Nevada's valuable minerals out of enemy hands. But there was a problem. To become a state, a territory had to have at least 127,381 people. Nevada had less than 20,000.

Despite the territory's low population, Nevadans drew up a state constitution. On October 31, 1864, the U.S. government made an exception and allowed Nevada to join the Union as the 36th state. Because it was admitted during the Civil War, Nevada has since been called the Battle Born State.

Nevada became a state in 1864. This stamp was issued in 1964, to celebrate Nevada's 100th year of statehood.

Native Americans forced onto reservations faced poverty and many other difficulties.

    As Nevada's population grew, the area's Indians were slowly forced off their lands. Some bands of Paiute, Shoshone, and Washo became hostile. They attacked miners and other settlers who had invaded Indian land.

    In the 1870s, lawmakers decided that Indians and settlers could not live side by side peacefully. The U.S. government set up areas of land called **reservations,** and the Indians were forced to move onto this land. The Indians were expected to stay on the reservations and to grow their own food. But they were used to their freedom. The Indians had a hard time living on reservations.

Miners pose in front of a mine at Pickhandle Gulch.

Mining in Nevada reached its peak during the 1870s. More than 40,000 people lived in the Silver State, mostly in Virginia City. But by the end of the decade, the U.S. government had begun to pay less money for silver. Mining in Nevada was no longer profitable.

Tens of thousands of people left the state. Nevada's population dropped by almost half. Some cities were completely abandoned, turning into ghost towns overnight.

In the 1800s, people going to or from Nevada sometimes traveled by stagecoach.

Nevada's vast grasslands attracted Basques *(below)* to the state to herd sheep *(inset)*.

Many people who stayed in Nevada started raising cattle. Others, mostly Basques (people from a region in Spain), settled in northern Nevada in the 1880s to herd sheep on the grasslands.

In 1900 silver was discovered at Tonopah.

Livestock ranching, however, was not nearly as profitable as mining silver or gold had been. Times were difficult for Nevada's ranchers, who paid high rates to ship their meat and wool by train to markets in the eastern United States.

Nevadans soon discovered that the Comstock Lode was not the only source of minerals in their state. In the early 1900s, prospectors found more deposits of gold, silver, and copper, and Nevada experienced another mining boom.

Nevada's farmers could better irrigate crops once the Newlands Irrigation Project, built near Reno, was completed.

Probably just as important as minerals to Nevadans was the completion of the Newlands Irrigation Project in 1907. The project, a system of dams built on the Truckee and Carson Rivers, stored water needed for irrigation. With a reliable source of water, farmers could grow more crops.

Throughout most of Nevada's mining days, **gambling,** or betting money on various games, had been popular. In 1910 the practice was outlawed.

Nevada's mining industry received a boost in 1917 when the United States entered World War I (1914–1918). Factories needed copper, zinc, and other metals to build weapons and military supplies. But prices fell after the war ended in 1918, and many mines closed.

In 1931 the state government again legalized gambling throughout Nevada—the only state at the time to have done so. Reno and other towns reopened their old gambling houses, called **casinos.** Once again, people were coming to Nevada to try and strike it rich.

Casinos drew crowds of people in the 1930s, when gambling in Nevada became legal again.

In 1936 workers finished Hoover Dam, one of the largest dams in the world. Located on the Colorado River, Hoover Dam stored water for irrigation, households, and businesses. The dam also used waterpower to generate electricity. Because Hoover Dam provided these services, surrounding communities, such as Las Vegas, could grow.

World War II (1939–1945) also helped the state's economy. Mining again flourished and new businesses brought in more wealth. After the war, the people of Nevada worked to bring in new industry. Nuclear research and tourism soon became essential to Nevada's economy.

Hoover Dam's construction took six years.

When the U.S. government tested atomic bombs in the 1950s, Nevadans could see giant clouds.

By 1950 about 160,000 people lived in Nevada, but much of the state was thinly populated. Partly for this reason, the U.S. government chose Nevada as a testing site for atomic bombs for use in warfare. Testing was needed to make sure the bombs worked and to study the effects of the explosions. Exploding bombs created mushroom-shaped clouds that could be seen for miles around.

Citizens soon feared the harmful effects of atomic bombs on people and the environment. In 1963 the tests were moved underground, where the effects were not as great and could be more easily measured. The government continues to test atomic devices underground.

Nevada's population is growing fast. Between 1990 and 2000, Nevada gained almost 800,000 new residents. These new houses are being built near Las Vegas.

In the 1970s and 1980s, tourism thrived. Las Vegas and Reno expanded their airports and other facilities to accommodate the increasing flood of visitors.

Tourism is still the state's number-one industry. In 2000 Nevada attracted nearly 50 million visitors, a state record. Las Vegas and Reno alone brought in $33 billion for the state.

Lately the Silver State is experiencing a new kind of boom. Between 1990 and 2000, the state's population grew by 66 percent, making Nevada the fastest-growing state in the nation.

PEOPLE & ECONOMY

Old and New Boomtowns

Silent saloons. Crumbling buildings. Long-deserted mines emptied of their treasures. Nevada's mining history lingers in the hundreds of ghost towns and abandoned mines located throughout the state. These towns are empty because most miners left once they had made their fortunes.

Many of Nevada's surviving smaller towns actually had more people during the 1800s or early 1900s than they have today. Virginia City, once the state's largest mining town, has become a tourist attraction with only about 1,000 residents. Goldfield, a mining town that once reached a population of 20,000, has only about 500 people.

This elegant house, built in Virginia City in 1868, is a reminder of Nevada's history of mining wealth. By the mid-1870s, Virginia City's population had grown to nearly 20,000 people.

Once a booming mining city,
Rochester is now a ghost town.

The true ghost towns of Nevada
are those without any residents.
Rhyolite, Hamilton, Delamar, and
Tybo are just a few of the many
deserted mining areas in Nevada.
Visitors can imagine decorated
storefronts and noisy saloons, hear
the sound of horses' hooves, and
picture the miners heading out to
their claims with picks in hand and
burros in tow.

Young Nevadans enjoy a day at a playground *(right)*. Basque dancers *(below)* celebrate the traditions of their Spanish ancestors.

The people of Nevada's past came from many parts of the world, but most present-day Nevadans are of European descent. About 6 percent of Nevadans are Latinos, with many recent **immigrants** arriving from Mexico. Native Americans make up about 1 percent of the population. Some live on the state's 21 Indian reservations. African Americans make up almost 7 percent of the population.

All of these people totaled nearly 2 million in 2000. Las Vegas, the state's largest city, has about 480,000 residents and more jobs than any other town in Nevada. Reno is the second biggest with about 180,000 people. Carson City, Nevada's capital, is home to more than 52,000. Less than one-fifth of the state's population lives in **rural** areas.

Compared to other states, Nevada ranks 35th in its permanent population. But when you add the number of visitors who arrive on any given day, Nevada's population can double in size.

Nevada's state capitol building in Carson City

Gambling attracts the majority of visitors to Nevada. In Las Vegas, brightly lit casinos line Las Vegas Boulevard, better known as the Strip. People try their luck 24 hours a day at blackjack, poker, keno, slot machines, and more. Nightclubs advertise dozens of concerts and shows. The cities of Reno, Elko, and Laughlin are also popular choices for gambling and other entertainment.

The neon signs of downtown Las Vegas light the way for gamblers and shoppers.

Visitors to Valley of Fire State Park can see ancient rock drawings.

Nevada also features several unique museums. The Liberace Museum in Las Vegas honors the piano player Liberace, who was a major attraction on the Strip during his lifetime. The musician's 75-foot-long fox-skin cape and a 50-pound rhinestone are among his many belongings on display.

History buffs can visit the Old Mormon Fort. Built in 1855 by Mormons, the fort is the oldest building in Las Vegas. In Overton, the Lost City Museum displays tools and pottery found at Pueblo Grande de Nevada. The Nevada State Museum in Carson City features an underground mine that tourists can explore.

Bristlecone pines grow in Great Basin National Park.

The U.S. government owns most of the land in Nevada—about 80 percent of it. But the government didn't establish the state's first national park until 1986. Great Basin National Park in eastern Nevada boasts ancient bristlecone pine trees, deep caverns, miles of lonesome trails, and the state's highest mountain peak—Boundary Peak (13,140 feet).

People can hike, rock climb, or ride horseback through Nevada's state parks, many of which are littered with uniquely shaped rocks. Nevada's lakes offer boating, swimming, and water skiing. Anglers can catch anything from catfish to walleye. Winter sports lovers can ski down the Sierra Nevada or ice-skate near the resorts of Lake Tahoe.

Fishers inspect their catch at Pyramid Lake *(above)*. A chair lift gives skiers a spectacular view of Lake Tahoe *(left)*.

More than 70 percent of Nevada's workers have jobs that help visitors and Nevadans alike. These workers have service jobs, helping people and businesses. Hotel desk clerks, nurses, and bank tellers all have service jobs.

The U.S. government employs 11 percent of Nevada's workforce. Nellis Air Force Base in southern Nevada employs more than 10,000 government workers.

Manufacturing is another important employer in Nevada. Factory workers make up about 4 percent of the workforce. Computers, medical equipment, lumber products, neon signs, and pet food are among the many products made in the state. Las Vegas, Reno, and Carson City have the largest number of manufacturing plants in Nevada.

Workers at Nellis Air Force Base check out a Navy EA-6B Prowler before its next flight.

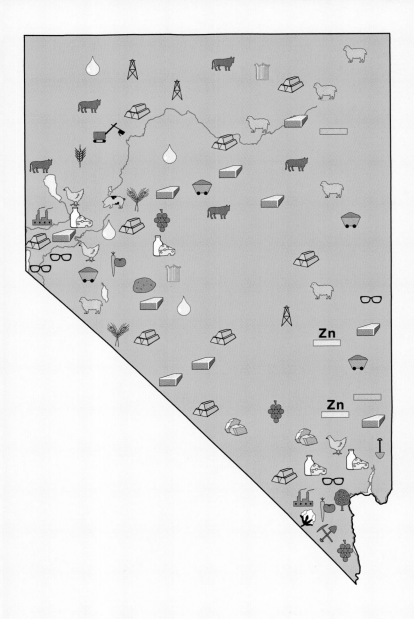

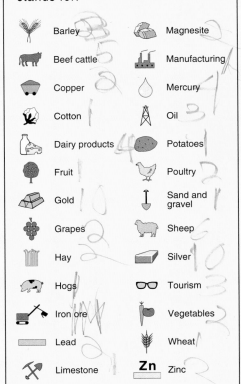

NEVADA
Economic Map

The symbols on this map show where different economic activities take place in Nevada. The legend below explains what each symbol stands for.

	Barley		Magnesite
	Beef cattle		Manufacturing
	Copper		Mercury
	Cotton		Oil
	Dairy products		Potatoes
	Fruit		Poultry
	Gold		Sand and gravel
	Grapes		Sheep
	Hay		Silver
	Hogs		Tourism
	Iron ore		Vegetables
	Lead		Wheat
	Limestone	**Zn**	Zinc

Modern cowboys still round up cattle in Nevada *(above)*. Gold is separated from ore at this northeastern Nevada mine *(above right)*.

Mining is not as big an industry as it was in the 1870s, when Nevada earned the nickname the Silver State. Still, Nevada ranks third in the world for producing gold, and it is a national leader in producing mercury and magnesite. Silver is still taken from the land, but gold now earns more money for the state. In northern Nevada, rigs drill for oil.

Livestock ranching has been a major industry in Nevada since the 1880s. Nevada has about 3,000 farms and ranches. Because of the small amount of rain in Nevada, most crops need to be irrigated. Hay, barley, potatoes, wheat, alfalfa, and grapes are some of the state's harvests.

THE ENVIRONMENT

Running Out of Water

Each year, thousands of people move to Nevada. Las Vegas has become the fastest-growing metropolitan area in the nation, taking in about 6,000 new residents each month. Many companies, attracted partly by low taxes and inexpensive land, are making Nevada their base. Nevada has become the fastest-growing state in the nation.

Nevada's growing population of young people relies on clean water.

Nevada is also the driest state in the country, receiving only 9 inches of precipitation each year. This does not supply the state with enough water, so people and crops must rely on water that has been stored away.

Storm clouds occasionally hover over Nevada, but rain is scarce in the state.

Power plants need large amounts of water to create electricity for Nevada's growing cities, such as Las Vegas *(left)*. Some of Nevada's water supply goes to irrigate farmland *(below)*.

Rivers are Nevada's most plentiful source of water. Hoover Dam was built on the Colorado River to store and supply water to parts of Nevada, Colorado, and Arizona. But the amount of water Hoover Dam can provide to farms, homes, and businesses is limited. Each state is allowed only so much water from the dam. If Nevada needs more than its share, Nevadans must look elsewhere for water.

Most of Nevada's water comes from rivers.

About 30 percent of the state's water comes from underneath the ground, where nature has stored it for centuries. Water collects underground when soil soaks up rain or snow. As it seeps into the ground, the water flows through cracks in rocks that lie below the surface of the earth. Over thousands of years, large pools of water, called **aquifers,** have formed underground.

Nevadans dig wells to pump the **groundwater** from nearby aquifers to croplands, homes, and factories. Wells have supplied tons of water to Nevada. As more and more groundwater is used, however, the water level in the aquifers gets lower and lower. Someday the aquifers may dry up completely.

A large factory might use more water in one day than you might use in your home in a lifetime. Some factories need tons of water to cool down machinery that is hot from operating for many hours. Other factories boil water to create steam heat. Water is also used to help make many products. Much of this water is not lost. It is used over and over again. But as more factories open in Nevada, more water is needed.

To reach water in aquifers, workers must drill underground.

Households also use a lot of water. Families need water to shower, flush the toilet, cook, and do laundry. Each person uses more than 100 gallons of water a day. With a population of

Getting an ice-cold drink is a great way to cool off on hot day. This is just one of the many ways that Nevadans use water in their households.

almost 2 million, Nevadans use at least 200 million gallons of water a day.

As Nevada's population grows, more people will need to use the state's limited water supply. To make sure farms, households, and businesses continue to have the water they need, Nevada must either use its water more wisely or find new sources.

One way to increase Nevada's water supply is to pipe or ship water in from other states that have more water than they need. Some of the northern states, especially Alaska, have plenty. But shipping or piping water into Nevada would be expensive. And other states are not always willing to give up their water.

Nevadans may need to go outside their state to get more water, but they can also make sure not to waste the water they do have. People can easily cut their water use by fixing leaking faucets, taking shorter showers, and sprinkling lawns less often. Factories can conserve water by using other methods to heat up or cool down machinery. They can also use less water to make products.

By lining irrigation canals and ditches with concrete, farmers prevent water from escaping. Watertight canals also keep weeds, which drink a lot of water, from growing along the paths of the canals. Farmers can also be careful not to give the plants in the fields too much water.

Concrete canals help conserve Nevada's usable water.

The people of Nevada know how important their water supply is. In southern Nevada, where most of the state's population resides, local agencies are striving to protect their water supply. In 1991 the Southern Nevada Water Authority was established. The Authority works to change water usage in southern Nevada through public education, free services, and other programs. These efforts are helping. By 1999 the Authority reported that southern Nevada had conserved 20.8 billion gallons of water.

More water than land covers the earth. The state of Nevada, however, has a very small fraction of the world's water supply. To meet growing needs for water, Nevadans must keep planning so they will have enough water for the future.

All Nevadans, whether they live in the country or in cities such as Reno *(above)*, can help conserve the state's water supply.

Fun Facts

Nevada's first speed limit was set in Tonopah in 1905. Cars in the town were not allowed to go faster than 4 miles per hour—the speed of a brisk walk.

Area 51, a military base in southern Nevada, was built in the 1950s to test spy planes. Over the years, however, the secret base and its surrounding area have been associated with rumors of Unidentified Flying Objects (UFOs). By 1996 there were so many stories about aliens at Area 51 that a highway running between Alamo and Tonopah, Nevada, was officially renamed the "Extraterrestrial Highway."

Some of the world's largest ichthyosaur fossils have been found near Berlin, Nevada. The prehistoric reptiles grew up to 60 feet long and 8 feet around.

In 1864 Reuel Gridley, a grocer from Austin, Nevada, wanted to raise money for the Civil War effort. He auctioned off the same 50-pound sack of flour over and over again for five months as a charity fundraiser, raising around $150,000. He gave the money to the U.S. Sanitary Commission, which later became the American Red Cross.

The last great western bank robbery was staged in Winnemucca, Nevada, on September 19, 1900. A gang called the Wild Bunch crept into town and made off with more than $32,000 from the First National Bank. The gang escaped to Wyoming on stolen horses.

The oldest living trees in the world—Great Basin bristlecone pine trees—are found in Nevada. Some of the evergreens are more than 4,000 years old.

STATE SONG

In 1932 Reno resident Bertha Raffetto was asked to sing a song about Nevada at a large picnic gathering. Finding no songs that expressed how she felt about the state, she wrote her own song and called it "Home Means Nevada." It was adopted as the official state song the next year.

HOME MEANS NEVADA

Words and music by Bertha Raffetto

Way out in the land of the set-ting sun, Where the wind blows wild and free, There's a love-ly spot, just the on - ly one That means home sweet home to me. If you fol - low the old Kit Car - son trail, Un - til des-ert meets the hills, Oh you cer-tain-ly will a-gree with me, It's the place of a thou-sand thrills.

Home means Ne-va - da, Home means the hills, Home means the sage and the pine.

Out by the Truck - ee, sil - ver - y rills, Out where the sun al - ways shines,

Here is the land which I love the best, Fair - er than all I can see.

Deep in the heart of the gold - en west Home means Ne-va - da to me.

You can hear "Home Means Nevada" by visiting this website:
<http://www.50states.com/songs/nevada.htm>

A NEVADA RECIPE

During a cattle drive, chuck wagons carried food and supplies for cooking—including a cook. For the cooks following cowboys across the open range, beans were an important food. Beans in a pot made up part of almost every supper on the range. Pinto beans were one of the most common types used on the range, but any bean will do. Serve as a tasty side dish with barbecued meat.

COWBOY BEANS

You will need:

2 15-ounce cans pinto beans, drained
1 14.5-ounce can whole tomatoes
1 tablespoon onion, minced
1 tablespoon chili powder

½ teaspoon black pepper
¼ teaspoon red pepper
4 slices of bacon, chopped

1. Ask an adult to preheat oven to 375° F.
2. Crush tomatoes with back of a spoon.
3. Combine all ingredients in a 2-quart casserole dish. Mix well.
4. With an adult's help, bake uncovered for 40 minutes.

Makes 8 servings.

HISTORICAL TIMELINE

10,000 B.C. The first people move into the Nevada area.

A.D. 100 Native Americans living in the region start raising crops.

750 Basket Makers begin irrigating crops and building pueblos.

1150 Pueblo Indians have abandoned the city of Pueblo Grande de Nevada.

1826 Peter Ogden and Jedediah Smith arrive in the Nevada area.

1848 The California gold rush brings miners through the Nevada region.

1851 Mormons establish Genoa, the first white settlement in the Nevada area.

1857 Mormons leave Genoa to return to Utah.

1859 The Comstock Lode is discovered.

1861 The U.S. government creates the Nevada Territory.

1864 Nevada becomes the 36th state.

1870s The U.S. government moves Native Americans onto reservations.

1880s The mining industry fails and thousands of people leave Nevada.

1907 Workers complete the Newlands Irrigation Project.

1910 Nevada outlaws gambling.

1917 Nevada's mining industry grows when the United States enters World War I (1914–1918).

1931 Nevada legalizes gambling.

1936 The construction of Hoover Dam is completed.

1950 The U.S. government begins testing atomic bombs in Nevada.

1963 Atomic testing in Nevada is moved underground.

2000 Nevada's tourist industry attracts a record-breaking 50 million visitors; census figures show that Nevada is the fastest-growing state in the nation.

OUTSTANDING NEVADANS

Eva Adams

Andre Agassi

Ben Alexander

James E. Casey

Eva Adams (1908–1991) was a businesswoman who began her career as a professor at the University of Nevada. From 1961 to 1969, she was director of the U.S. Mint, where she supervised the making and storing of coins. Adams also worked as a business consultant, teaching supervisors how to better manage their employees. She was born in Wonder, Nevada.

Andre Agassi (born 1970) is a tennis player from Las Vegas. Agassi has won more than 45 singles titles and 6 major titles. His popularity skyrocketed in the late 1980s when he became known for his flair on and off the court. After a brief slump in the mid-1990s, Agassi revived his career after winning the U.S. Open.

Ben Alexander (1911–1969) was a television and movie actor. His most famous role was police officer Frank Smith on the television series *Dragnet* from 1953 to 1959. Alexander, who was born Nicholas Benton Alexander, was from Garfield, Nevada.

Helen Delich Bentley (born 1923) is a businesswoman and politician who began her career with the *Baltimore Sun* newspaper. In 1969 she was appointed chairwoman of the Federal Maritime Commission, making her the highest-ranking woman in the federal government and the first woman to be appointed head of a regulatory agency. She was born in Ruth, Nevada.

James E. Casey (1888–1983) was a businessman who founded United Parcel Service (UPS) in 1907. UPS has grown to be one of the largest independent delivery services in the world. Casey was born in Candelaria, Nevada.

Glen Charles (born 1943) and **Les Charles** (born 1948) are writers from Henderson, Nevada. They have written for and produced several successful television series, including *M*A*S*H*, *Taxi*, and *Cheers*. Working as a team, the two brothers have won more than a dozen awards for their scripts.

Glen (right) and Les Charles

Walter van Tilburg Clark (1909–1971), a writer and poet, is famous for his western novels. Two of his books, *The Ox-Bow Incident* and *Track of the Cat*, were made into movies. Clark also wrote several nonfiction books about Nevada. He grew up in Reno, Nevada.

Samuel Clemens (1835–1910) was a writer who lived in Nevada in the early 1860s. He wrote for the *Territorial Enterprise*, the Virginia City newspaper where he began using the pen name Mark Twain. *Roughing It* is a famous story the author wrote about his adventures in Nevada.

Samuel Clemens

Henry Comstock (1820–1870) was a miner living in Nevada in 1859, when a group of miners found silver on land he claimed to own. He gained large shares of the deposits, which became known as the Comstock Lode.

Henry Comstock

Abby Dalton (born 1932), of Las Vegas, is an actress who played Julia Cumson on the television show *Falcon Crest*, which was popular in the 1980s. Dalton has appeared in several other series, including *Barney Miller*.

Dat-So-La-Lee (1835?–1925) was a Washo Indian basket weaver who lived in Carson Valley, Nevada. Some of her baskets took months to make and are worth thousands of dollars. Her art is displayed at several museums around the country, including the Nevada State Museum in Carson City.

Dat-So-La-Lee

Sarah Winnemucca Hopkins

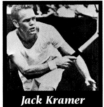

Jack Kramer

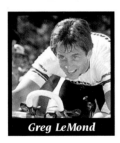

Greg LeMond

Pat Nixon

Sarah Winnemucca Hopkins (1844?–1891) was an activist for Native American rights. Hopkins, a Paiute Indian, was the first Native American woman to publish a book. In 1884 she established the first school for Indian children in Nevada. She was born near Humboldt Lake.

Jack Kramer (born 1921) was a popular tennis player in the 1940s. He won the U.S. Open in 1946 and 1947 and won the All-England Championship at Wimbledon in 1947. Kramer is from Las Vegas.

Greg LeMond (born 1961), a professional cyclist, grew up in Nevada's Washoe Valley. In 1986 he became the first American to win the Tour de France. LeMond has won the Tour de France three times and the World Professional Championship twice. In 1989 he became the fourth person to win both races in the same year. He retired from cycling in 1994 and started his own line of bikes.

John William Mackay (1831–1902) was a miner who became rich after his crew struck a huge vein of gold and silver ore in Virginia City. The Big Bonanza, as it was called, produced more than $100 million worth of minerals for Mackay and his partners.

Greg Maddux (born 1966) is a major-league baseball pitcher for the Atlanta Braves. Maddux has won the Cy Young award four years in a row (1992–1995) and the Gold Glove Award 11 times. He grew up in Las Vegas.

Pat Nixon (1912–1993), first lady from 1969 to 1974, was born Thelma Catherine Ryan on Saint Patrick's Day in Ely, Nevada. Because of her birthday, her father nicknamed her Pat. In 1940 she married Richard Nixon, who later became president of the United States. As first lady, Pat urged Americans to do volunteer work.

Edna Purviance (1895–1958), an actress, starred in many of Charlie Chaplin's silent movies, including *The Tramp* and *Easy Street*. Purviance was born in Paradise Valley, Nevada, and grew up in Lovelock.

Edna Purviance

Benjamin "Bugsy" Seigel (1905–1947) was a gangster who moved to Las Vegas from New York to build the Flamingo Hotel. The hotel and casino opened in 1946 and cost Seigel $6 million. It was equipped with a maze of secret escape hatches and tunnels for gangster-style getaways. A motion picture about Seigel's life, entitled *Bugsy*, was released in 1991.

Benjamin "Bugsy" Seigel

William P. Sharon (1821–1885) was a powerful banker who gained control of many of Nevada's wealthiest mines. He and others in Nevada's so-called "Bank Crowd" became rich quickly. From 1875 to 1881, Sharon served as a U.S. senator from Nevada.

William P. Sharon

Jerry Tarkanian (born 1930) coached the Runnin' Rebels basketball team at the University of Nevada in Las Vegas for 19 seasons. They won an average of 83 percent of the games they played, the highest percentage of any college basketball coach. Tarkanian left the Rebels in 1992 and briefly coached the San Antonio Spurs. Since 1995 he has coached the Fresno State Bulldogs.

Wovoka (1856?–1932), also known as Jack Wilson, was a Paiute Indian religious leader born in Esmeralda County, Nevada. He originated the Ghost Dance, a religion which taught that starvation, sickness, and death could be avoided if people stopped fighting. Wovoka's ideas spread to many tribes throughout the West before losing popularity in the late 1890s.

Wovoka

FACTS-AT-A-GLANCE

Nickname: Silver State

Song: "Home Means Nevada"

Motto: All for Our Country

Flower: sagebrush

Tree: single-leaf piñon and bristlecone pine

Bird: mountain bluebird

Precious gemstone: black fire opal

Semi-precious gemstone: turquoise

Reptile: desert tortoise

Fossil: ichthyosaur

Fish: Lahontan cutthroat trout

Date and ranking of statehood:
 October 31, 1864, the 36th state

Capital: Carson City

Area: 109,806 square miles

Rank in area, nationwide: 7th

Average January temperature: 30° F

Average July temperature: 73° F

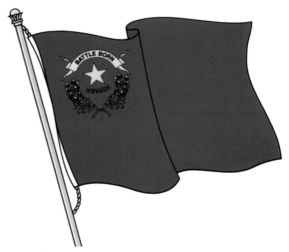

Nevada's state flag features sprigs of sagebrush (the state flower) and a silver star symbolizing the state's mineral wealth. The words "Battle Born" signify Nevada's admission to the Union during the Civil War.

POPULATION GROWTH

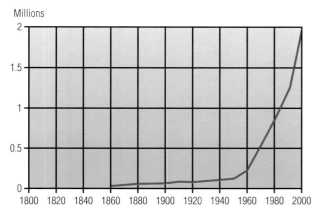

Millions

This chart shows how Nevada's population has grown from 1860 to 2000.

Nevada's state seal, adopted in 1866, depicts a railroad and telegraph line to represent the state's importance as a link between the East and the West Coast. The cart, tunnel, and mill stand for Nevada's mining industry, and the plow, sickle, and wheat represent agriculture.

Population: 1,998,257 (2000 census)

Rank in population, nationwide: 35th

Major cities and populations: (2000 census) Las Vegas (478,434), Reno (180,480), Henderson (175,381), North Las Vegas (115,488), Sparks (66,346)

U.S. senators: 2

U.S. representatives: 3

Electoral votes: 5

Natural resources: coal, copper, gold, iron ore, lead, limestone, magnesite, mercury, oil, salt, sand and gravel, silver

Agricultural products: alfalfa, barley, beef cattle, grapes, hay, onions, potatoes, sheep, wheat, wool

Mining industry: brucite, coal, copper, gold, lead, mercury, oil, silver, uranium, zinc

Manufactured goods: chemicals, computers, concrete, electronic equipment, food products, lumber products, medical equipment, neon signs, pet food, plastic, printed materials

WHERE NEVADANS WORK

Services—73 percent (services includes jobs in trade; community, social, and personal services; finance, insurance, and real estate; transportation, communication, and utilities)

Government—11 percent

Construction—9 percent

Manufacturing—4 percent

Agriculture—2 percent

Mining—1 percent

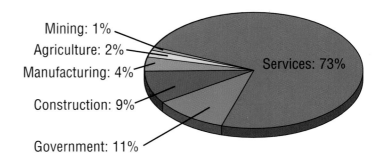

Mining: 1%
Agriculture: 2%
Manufacturing: 4%
Construction: 9%
Government: 11%
Services: 73%

GROSS STATE PRODUCT

Services—70 percent

Government—10 percent

Construction—10 percent

Manufacturing—5 percent

Mining—4 percent

Agriculture—1 percent

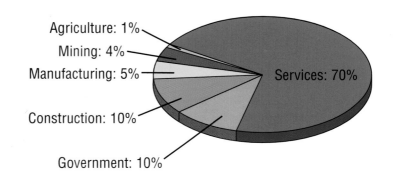

Agriculture: 1%
Mining: 4%
Manufacturing: 5%
Construction: 10%
Government: 10%
Services: 70%

NEVADA WILDLIFE

Mammals: badger, bighorn sheep, burro, coyote, fox, gray wolf, horse, mink, mule deer, muskrat, porcupine, pronghorn antelope, rabbit, raccoon

Birds: bald eagle, chukar partridge, duck, mountain bluebird, peregrine falcon, pelican, pheasant, quail, sage hen, tern

Amphibians and reptiles: desert iguana, desert tortoise, great basin whiptail, long-nosed leopard lizard, rattlesnake, tiger salamander, western toad

Fish: bass, carp, catfish, chub, crappie, cui-ui, trout

Trees: alder, aspen, bristlecone pine, cottonwood, fir, hemlock, juniper, spruce, willow

Wild plants: bitter brush, cactus, desert lily, mesquite, Indian paintbrush, larkspur, rabbit brush, sagebrush, shadscale, shooting star, violet, yucca

Ring-necked pheasants make homes on the grasslands in some parts of Nevada.

PLACES TO VISIT

Children's Museum of Northern Nevada, Carson City
This interactive museum features exhibits for all ages. Special displays include an air machine, an archaeological exhibit, and science displays to teach visitors about the universe.

Ethel M. Chocolate Factory & Cactus Garden, Henderson
Learn all about how chocolates are made. The factory also includes a three-acre botanical cactus garden, the largest in Nevada, with more than 300 species of cactuses.

Fleischmann Planetarium and Science Center, Reno
The planetarium features star shows and films, as well as a public observatory. The Science Center houses a collection of meteorites, including four recovered in Nevada, a model of Stonehenge, and scales that help visitors learn their weight on different planets.

Hoover Dam, Boulder City
Completed in 1936, Hoover Dam is one of the highest concrete dams in the world. Exhibits, presentations, and guided tours are available.

Great Basin National Park, near Baker
Great Basin features diverse landscapes, from desert basins to glacier-topped mountain peaks. Park visitors can explore Lehman Caves, hike miles of trails, camp, fish, or see the oldest living thing on the planet—a pine tree dated at almost 5,000 years old.

Liberace Museum, Las Vegas

Visitors to the museum can check out memorabilia from the world-famous pianist. The collection includes a rare piano collection and samples from his glittering wardrobe.

Old Mormon Fort Historic Park, Las Vegas

This site of the first settlement of Las Vegas was built in 1855. The fort's remains are the oldest European-American building in Nevada. The site includes a visitor's center and historic programs.

Nevada State Museum, Carson City

This museum features exhibits about Nevada's history, geology, and culture. Main attractions include a walk-through ghost town and an underground mine.

Rhyolite Historic Site, Beatty

Considered one of the most famous ghost towns in the state, attractions at Rhyolite include the old railroad depot and an open-air museum.

Virginia City

Learn more about Nevada's mining industry with a visit to its most famous boomtown. Attractions include underground mines, historic buildings, mansions, and miners' cemeteries. Museums include Marshall Mint and Museum, Nevada Gambling Museum, and Territorial Enterprise Mark Twain Museum.

ANNUAL EVENTS

Cowboy Poetry Gathering, Elko—*January–February*

Henderson Heritage Days, Henderson—*April*

Carson Valley Days, Carson Valley—*June*

Laughlin River Days, Laughlin—*June*

ARTown, Reno—*July*

National Basque Festival, Elko—*July*

Harvest Festival, Las Vegas—*August*

Nevada State Fair, Reno—*August*

Nevada Shakespeare Festival, Virginia City—*September–October*

Magical Forest, Las Vegas—*November–December*

Parade of Lights, Boulder City—*December*

LEARN MORE ABOUT NEVADA

BOOKS

General

Fradin, Dennis Brindell. *Nevada.* Chicago: Children's Press, 1998. For older readers.

Stefoff, Rebecca. *Nevada.* New York: Benchmark Books, 2001. For older readers.

Stein, R. Conrad. *Nevada.* New York: Children's Press, 2000.

Special Interest

Collins, David. *Mark T-W-A-I-N: A Story about Samuel Clemens.* Minneapolis: Carolrhoda Books, 1993. This biography covers the life of American humorist Mark Twain, including the time he spent at Virginia City's *Territorial Enterprise* newspaper.

Doherty, Craig A., and Katherine M. Doherty. *Hoover Dam.* Woodbridge, CT: Blackbirch Marketing, 1995. This book covers the four-year development of the famous dam.

Gutman, Bill. *Greg Lemond.* Austin, TX: Raintree/Steck Vaughn, 1998. This biography covers the life, training, and obstacles of the first American to win the Tour de France bicycle race.

Johnson, Rebecca. *A Walk in the Desert.* Minneapolis: Carolrhoda Books, 2000. Read more about the plants and animals that live in the deserts of North America.

Fiction

Kelso, Mary Jean. *Abducted!* Springfield, OR: Markel Press, 1988. Lynne Garrett returns to Nevada to be in a friend's wedding. But plans go awry when her friend is abducted.

Lasky, Kathryn. *Alice Rose and Sam.* New York: Hyperion Books, 1998. Twelve-year-old Alice Rose gets more than her share of adventure when she teams up with Mark Twain, a reporter for her father's Virginia City newspaper. For older readers.

Levinson, Nancy Smiler. *Snowshoe Thompson.* New York: HarperCollins, 1992. John Thompson braves the ice and snow of the Sierra Nevada Mountains to create a path for other people to travel.

Yep, Laurence. *Dragon's Gate.* New York: HarperCollins, 1993. Otter, a young Chinese immigrant, flees to the Sierra Nevada, where thousands of immigrants are carving a path for the railroad. For older readers.

WEBSITES

State of Nevada
<http://www.silver.state.nv.us/>
The state's official website features information about Nevada's history, businesses, and government.

Nevada Commission on Tourism
<http://www.travelnevada.com>
Learn more about the Silver State's attractions, including museums, events, and historical sites.

Las Vegas Review-Journal
<http://www.lvrj.com/>
Read about current events in the state and the world in the online version of Las Vegas's biggest newspaper.

Nevada State Museum
<http://www.dmla.clan.lib.nv.us/docs/museums/tour/>
Take a virtual tour of the museum, which is in Carson City, and see the full-sized replica of a ghost town and an underground mine.

PRONUNCIATION GUIDE

Basques (BASKS)

Genoa (juh-NOH-uh)

Lahontan (luh-HAHN-tuhn)

Paiute (PY-yoot)

Rhyolite (RY-uh-lyt)

Shoshone (shuh-SHOHN)

Sierra Nevada (see-EHR-uh nuh-VAD-uh)

Tahoe (TAH-hoh)

Tonopah (TOHN-uh-pah)

Winnemucca (wihn-uh-MUHK-uh)

Lake Mead is an artificial lake created by Hoover Dam's restriction of the Colorado River.

GLOSSARY

aquifer: an underground layer of rock, sand, or gravel containing water that can be drawn out for use above ground

casino: a place where people gamble

desert: an area that receives about 10 inches or less of rain or snow a year

flash flood: a sudden, short-lived flood that usually occurs after a heavy rain

gambling: placing bets (usually money) on games such as poker or dice

ghost town: a town that was once booming but has since been deserted because a natural resource such as gold or silver has been used up

groundwater: water that lies beneath the earth's surface

immigrant: a person who moves into a foreign country and settles there

irrigation: a method of watering land by directing water through canals, ditches, pipes, or sprinklers

lava: hot, melted rock that erupts from a volcano or from cracks in the earth's surface and that hardens as it cools

mesa: an isolated hill with steep sides and a flat top

plateau: a large, relatively flat area that stands above the surrounding land

precipitation: rain, snow, and other forms of moisture that fall to earth

pueblo: any of the ancient Indian villages in the southwestern United States with buildings of stone or clay, usually built one above the other. The word *Pueblo* also refers to an Indian tribe that lives in the Southwest.

reservation: public land set aside by the government to be used by Native Americans

reservoir: a place where water is collected and stored for later use

rural: having to do with the countryside or farming

INDEX

PHOTO ACKNOWLEDGMENTS

Cover photographs by © Richard Cummins/CORBIS (both); PresentationMaps.com, pp. 1, 8, 9, 49; © Jan Butchofsky-Houser/CORBIS, pp. 2–3; © Pat O'Hara/CORBIS, p. 3; © Ken Lucas/Visuals Unlimited, pp. 4 (detail), 7 (detail), 17 (detail), 39 (detail), 51 (detail); © Howard Folsom/Photo Network, p. 6; David Matherly/Visuals Unlimited, pp. 10, 11; Lake Tahoe Visitors Authority, pp. 12, 47 (bottom); James Blank/Root Resources, p. 13; Doyen Salsig, pp. 14, 16 (right), 19, 32 (inset), 41, 55; Anthony Mercieca/Root Resources, p. 16 (left); Patrick Cone, pp. 17 (right), 50 (right), 61; *Pine Tree Ceremonial Dance*, by José Rey Toledos, University of Oklahoma Museum of Art, Norman, Oklahoma, p. 20; Pueblo Grande de Nevada Collection, University of Nevada, Las Vegas Library, Spec. Coll. Neg. #0143 0484, p. 21; Smithsonian Institution National Anthropological Archives, Bureau of American Ethnology Collection, Neg. No. 1633, p. 22; Nevada Historical Society, pp. 25, 26, 27, 29, 31, 32 (top), 67 (top), 68 (bottom), 69 (top); Mystic Stamp Company, p. 28; W. H. Shockley Collection, University of Nevada, Las Vegas Library, Special Collections, Neg. #0241 0002, p. 30; Special Collections, University of Nevada—Reno Library, pp. 33, 69 (second from bottom); National Archives, p. 34; Gladys Frazier Collection, University of Nevada, Las Vegas Library, Special Collections, Neg. #0039 0006, p. 35; Library of Congress, p. 36; Las Vegas News Bureau, p. 37; © Richard Cummins/CORBIS, p. 38; Kent & Donna Dannen, pp. 40, 45, 52; © Mark E. Gibson/Visuals Unlimited, p. 42 (top); Nevada Commission on Tourism, p. 42 (bottom); Department of General Services, p. 43; © Larry Dunmire/Photo Network, p. 44; National Park Service, p. 46; Jeff Greenberg, pp. 47 (top), 50 (left), 55; U.S. Air Force, p. 48; © Tom McCarthy/Photo Network, p. 51; © Buddy Mays/Travel Stock, pp. 53 (left), 59; Nevada Division of Water Planning, pp. 53 (right), 54, 58; © D. Yeske/Visuals Unlimited, p. 56; Jack Lindstrom, p. 60; Tim Seeley, pp. 63, 71 (top), 72; UNLV Collection, University of Nevada, Las Vegas Library, p. 66 (top); © Duomo/CORBIS, p. 66 (second from top); Photofest, p. 66 (second from bottom); United Parcel Service, p. 66 (bottom); Cheers, p. 67 (top); *Dictionary of American Portraits*, pp. 67 (second from top, second from bottom); International Tennis Hall of Fame and Tennis Museum at the Newport Casino, Newport, Rhode Island, p. 68 (second from top); Darcy Kiefel/Kiefel Sportfolio, p. 68 (second from bottom); Nixon Presidential Materials Project, p. 68 (bottom); Flamingo Hilton, p. 69 (second from top); Bureau of American Ethnology Collection, National Anthropological Archives, Smithsonian Institution, p. 69 (bottom); Jean Matheny, p. 70 (top); Ron Nichols/USDA, p. 73; A. A. M. Van Der Heyden/IPS, p. 80.